Making Light Work of Workday

Strategies for unleashing
the power of Workday

STEPHEN SLEVIN   **DANIEL DORE**

R^ethink

First published in Great Britain in 2022
by Rethink Press (www.rethinkpress.com)

'Lightbulb' icon by Adrien Coquet, from
thenounproject.com

The SAHARA Model® (word and figurative) is a
registered trademark of Daniel James Dore.

The authors will donate all their royalties from
sales of this book to Motor Neurone Disease
Association (www.mndassociation.org).

Contents

Introduction

We know from our experience that many leaders of change struggle to implement the full benefits of the Workday platform and, despite their commitment and financial investment, they feel they're not realising its full potential. Our response is that there is a way forward, and as complex as Workday may seem, the solution is a relatively simple one. Our purpose in writing this book is to reconnect you with, and reignite, that initial enthusiasm for the platform.

We are passionate about Workday and its abilities to transform strategic decision-making.

As boutique independent service partners, we've witnessed how many businesses, despite their commitment and financial investment, feel they're not realising Workday's full potential and become disheartened when the outcomes they were hoping for fail to materialise in meaningful ways. Our purpose in writing this book is to share our passion with readers who are familiar with Workday's products but struggle to implement the benefits of the platform. As complex as it may seem, there is a way forward, and the solution is relatively simple.

If you haven't yet used the product and would like to know more about how Workday can help your business thrive, this book is also for you. Workday is a system software company that puts people and projects at the centre of business, bringing finance, HR and planning together to achieve deeper insight and greater functionality. By arming yourself with our extensive knowledge about the dos and don'ts of how to use the platform, you will be in the best position to benefit from its many sophisticated features.

We will offer you a roadmap which leads to the outcomes you originally hoped for, putting *you* at the centre of bringing about transformational strategic change in the business and delivering the all-important return on investment (ROI). We understand the constant scrutiny you're under to prove the value of Workday and the frustration you feel in it not living up to expectations. After all, it's a premium product and all eyes are on you to justify its expense, especially when peers in your industry sector appear to be implementing it successfully.

Those leaders have achieved success by ensuring the foundations are in place for Workday to serve their users. They are compliant and meet regulation requirements and they always adopt the latest Workday releases to maintain the maximum value from the platform, increasing its functionality and unlocking incredible insights from their data sets that inform and drive strategic decisions. They are at the vanguard of their business community and are viewed as agents of change, while you're left wondering, 'What am I doing wrong?' Even with a Workday software implementation partner (SI) in place, progress is slow and not much of that feels entirely relevant to your business.

Our frontline experience with customers who've fallen out of love with Workday prompted us to drill down and consider these problems in detail from the client perspective. The following chapters contain our solutions. Many of the issues people experience with Workday are the same and usually stem from basic hurdles around matters of organising, reporting, data accuracy and the time these take. Although the recovery process could take at least twelve months to implement, don't be disheartened – you will soon begin to see progress.

We want this book to prompt you to think about the problems you experience with Workday. Why do your analytics fail to deliver the insights it promises? What's preventing you from fully augmenting and adopting all its powerful features? We also want you to question whether your organisation has instilled any formal governance that then aligns with initiatives and strategy. By unravelling Workday's perceived complexities, you'll unleash its full value. The good news is that you don't need a PhD in software development to do this, you simply need to be good at what you already do.

The book's structure

To get to grips with Workday over the first twelve months, we encourage clients to embed and follow our Lightwork 3A Blueprint™[1]:

- Lightwork Amplify

- Lightwork Augment

- Lightwork Analytics

The book is structured around the first two of these parts. In Part One: Amplify, we will show you how to reignite your excitement for Workday and build newfound confidence in its capabilities. By laying down these firm foundations, you will gain a powerful understanding of what's required to drive the major change described in Part Two: Augment. There, we will enlighten you on how to save time and money while building even bigger business value as a transformational leader. Throughout, we will offer wisdom drawn from our own experience, insights and case studies, and you will find 'lightbulb moments' – key points for you to reflect on. We will look at

---

[1] The SAHARA model and its affiliated solutions/platforms are (registered) trademarks.

operational analytics in Part One, but owing to the extensive nature of the subject, we won't delve into the advanced Lightwork Analytics of the 3A Blueprint here – this will be the topic of a separate volume.

We end the book with an extended case study from one of our clients whose experience and journey with Workday typifies many who gain momentum by following our 3A Blueprint. We want its positive outcomes to reconnect you with the vision you originally had for Workday, to illustrate how that vision works in practice and show you the benefits it can bring to every organisation. Through the whole business of forming, storming, norming and performing,[2] and pushing your teams, you'll see huge smiles on your employees' faces because they now feel a part of a business journey and they're doing something that affects the vision and culture of the business. That sense of governance brings ownership and accountability. None of these are carbon copy outcomes since every business is unique in its make-up, in how it sets

---

2   'Forming, Storming, Norming, and Performing: Tuckman's model for nurturing a team to high performance', Mind Tools (no date), www.mindtools.com/pages/article/newLDR_86.htm, accessed August 2022

its KPIs and strategic objectives. However, the principles that underlie the Workday journey – as outlined on our website portal https://lightwork.global/lw247 – remain the same.

The hidden theme

The book contains a hidden theme that will become apparent as you move through the chapters. When it does reveal itself, it will change your perception of Workday and you'll realise that the solution to your struggles has been hiding in plain sight the whole time. The simple methodologies contained within the book are designed to tell stories that highlight the hidden message.

This Workday companion book isn't the definitive step-by-step guide to using Workday. It's more about the vision that answers the 'why'. Knowing the right questions is key. Being able to reflect, then act on what the desired outcomes are, relies on you knowing what it is that Workday can deliver to you – not the other way around. That shift in mindset is key to its success... and to yours.

1

The Workday Digital Transformation Journey

We have spoken with hundreds of HR leaders in the UK, the USA and Australia about Workday, and discovered that the digital transformation is far more predictable than anyone realises. There is a common journey that organisations go on that presents the same problems, in the same order, time and time again. The solutions are also predictable, and you can find mini industries dedicated to fixing these problems if you know what you're looking for. The Workday digital transformation journey includes six phases.

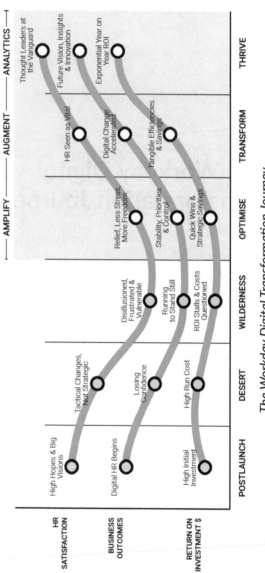

The Workday Digital Transformation Journey

Postlaunch

Every Workday journey typically begins as a silver bullet in the minds of leaders who want to digitally transform the way they work. Workday is a significant investment, but the prospect of rewards and benefits is substantial, and an ROI is fully expected. A leader will rightly have high aspirations for all that Workday can do for them, and user enthusiasm and morale spikes after the launch of this beautiful new feature-rich platform with brilliant potential outcomes. There is excitement, nervousness and anticipation.

Desert

When reality bites for the unprepared leader, Workday is the equivalent of a top-end sports car or thoroughbred horse. It outperforms the rest but only when it is cared for, maintained and fine-tuned. Within six to twelve months after the launch, Workday post-system environments can end up in survival mode, with leaders feeling lost and alone. The euphoria and excitement have dissipated; project teams have been disbanded. There's no specialist team to do the ongoing housekeeping and offer support, and Workday updates quickly become tactical rather than strategic, with regular upgrades missed. The leader spends all day hearing about day-to-day operational issues instead of new insights and starts to lose confidence in the product. At the same time, Workday running costs remain high and technical debt increases. The default solution is to throw money at the problem.

Wilderness

Around twelve to twenty-four months after a Workday launch, cracks start appearing, people start to grumble and expensive Workday consultants are called in to make all the problems go away – but they are only sticking plasters, treating symptoms and not the cause. The leader is now feeling disillusioned, frustrated and vulnerable. The ROI that Workday was due to deliver has stalled and senior stakeholders are starting to question its worth. Workday users, unknowingly in the wilderness, are not seeing the promised new features, and 'Who made the decision to buy Workday?' can be heard. The health of data and processes plummets along with people's faith and, critically, people disengage from Workday, which is fatal. It feels like an easy decision for the leader to yield to the pressure and abandon Workday, but that would be a huge mistake. There is a route out of the wilderness.

Optimise

The answer is to engage a small, dynamic, self-organised team with lower costs, Workday and HR specialisms and high-energy forms to establish stability, priorities and control. Quick wins and strategic savings are made. Workday realigns with the needs and outcomes of users, who now feel more confident, empowered and energised. For the leader, the dark clouds lift, the sense of relief is palpable, stress levels fall and they regain their freedom. This is an exciting time, when HR or finance are more visible and have greater kudos than ever.

Transform

Leaders are now agents of change across their organisation and their place at the top table is considered vital. The digital transformation journey is accelerating, and the culture, systems and processes shift up a gear. Workday user satisfaction and engagement skyrocket. Benefits are being realised beyond HR, with tangible efficiencies and savings in all areas of the business. A unique, dynamic team of professionals squeeze every drop of juice out of Workday, the business function is almost unrecognisable from the Workday launch team and they're enjoying every second.

Thrive

This is a performance team for organisations of the future, boldly stepping into the next industrial revolution. With Workday at the axis, organisations are dynamic, agile and incredibly fast. Nearly all decisions are data driven, AI and machine learning is normal, and an organisation's data becomes a profit centre rather than a cost. The future vision, insights and innovation delivered for the business leaders create competitive advantages they could previously only dream of. The digital transformation brings exponential year-on-year ROI: suddenly Workday feels like a bargain. 'Who made the decision to buy

Workday?' It was the leader at the cutting edge of their industry. A thought leader gaining outside attention and recognition – thriving.

An understanding of these predictable phases can guide you towards the ultimate goal, if you're a business leader with a level head. Your real choice is how high to shoot. **Optimise** is easily achievable with a little know-how. **Transform** takes dedication and **Thrive** needs an organisation ready for the challenge at all levels. One thing is for certain: no one wants to sweat it out in the **Desert** or be left wandering alone in the **Wilderness**.

Organisations follow predictable phases along the Workday digital transformation journey and most problems can be addressed quickly. Time is of the essence, as procrastination can cause unnecessary failure. By the end of this book, you'll have a clear strategy for building a Workday ecosystem that is optimised, transformational and thriving. Take the Lightwork Thriving on Workday Quiz at (https://thrivingonworkday.scoreapp.com) and find out where you are on the Workday digital transformation journey.

PART ONE

AMPLIFY

S I — *software implementation partner*

The problems organisations encounter with Workday typically follow some months after it has been purchased and implemented in their business. During that period, they've invested time in getting to know its functionality and capabilities, supported by their SI. The future looks great and the leader responsible for the purchase allows themselves a small pat on the back. All project, resources and Workday delivery partners are available to help design, build and test the system up until deployment. This is called the honeymoon period, when excitement is running high, along with expectations about what Workday will deliver to the business in the coming years. After all, the software enjoys an exceptional reputation and other organisations can't praise it enough. The original purchasing decision had been informed by a number of desired outcomes, principally:

- Slicker HR/finance efficiencies and processes

- New and insightful reporting that will inform operational processes and strategy

- The capability to shape the HR/finance and target operating model (TOM)

- Analysis and improvement on the organisation's cultural make-up

- Identification of business process inefficiencies

- The promise of ongoing functionality to support the business in an ever-changing world

The leader had been hoping that by implementing Workday they would be considered as the driving force of change within the organisation. They wanted new ways of working.

Why, then, is this leader struggling to see those same amazing results within their own business? Something doesn't seem to be working for them as efficiently as in other organisations, and now they're left wondering if all they've achieved is purchasing an expensive 'white elephant' that's not much better than the system they had before. They've hit a brick wall and can't see the wood for the trees. Simple issues become magnified out of all proportion, and this is then compounded by the biannual Workday functionality releases that are designed to assist continual improvement. Leaders tell us that at this stage they feel the sand slipping away beneath their feet; they are grinding to a halt.

The real tragedy of this is those organisations who, by not releasing the benefits from the biannual upgrades, are missing out on fantastic new functionality and insights. Many don't realise that Workday provides a significant number of additional resources as part of its licence subscription package, which would resolve many issues relatively quickly. Customers are then being challenged by senior leadership on their decision to commit to a costly overhead and the honeymoon is over.

In our experience, the problems that leaders encounter with Workday stem not from the functionality or capability of the software, but from within the organisation itself. We've identified a six-point firm foundation 'checklist' that, when applied continually from the outset, will provide leaders with a roadmap to successful, insightful and powerful accelerators for change. We will help demystify the perceived complexities of Workday and describe how leaders who were left feeling unsupported after the departure of a Workday SI can regain their optimism: like an oasis of clear water ahead of them, our SAHARA model offers an action plan of logical next steps followed by incremental changes to realise the desired outcomes. Of course, large multinational organisations with deep pockets can commit significant sums of money to hiring expensive consultants to do that for them. For a leader running a tight-knit department and budget, those same resources are not usually an option.

We've discovered that the reason people struggle with Workday is because they've skipped the first stage in our Lightwork Blueprint – Amplify – but it's at this stage that the solid foundations are set from which they'll be able to act and manage Workday successfully. Here, we set out our tried-and-tested methodology for doing this – SAHARA – which will have huge transformational impacts on your business. One of those impacts is how you can be more in control of Workday and how it can deliver for you so that you can step into the realm of the true service leader.

Amplify Accelerator®
Supercharged Workday ecosystems.

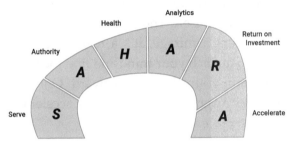

The SAHARA Model

Laying the foundations of the SAHARA model is the start of gaining the insights into that process. This is achieved in the following stages:

- **S**erve
- **A**uthority
- **H**ealth
- **A**nalytics
- **R**eturn on investment
- **A**ccelerate

The first step is to return to base and begin with some basic maintenance, and the first part of Amplify looks at how we can help you unpick Workday with greater clarity to maximise its benefits. We will begin with the role you currently play – and who else you need working alongside you as you navigate the edge of this desert. The oasis we've mentioned above isn't a mirage, it's a real place where you can quench your thirst and find the means to sustain yourself going forward. Only then will the Augment and Analytics accelerators fall into place.

2
Serve

Our mission is to help organisations fall back in love with Workday. To some business leaders, that might only seem possible if they commit to finding a significant budget to spend on expensive further training or hiring in costly consultants. While that may be a logical next step, it fails to inspire, and it fails to get to the heart of why they have lost faith in the product in the first place. The white elephant remains, and nobody wants to admit the possibility that they've made a mistake by introducing it into the organisation. It felt like the right decision at the time, but its appearance has left most people mystified as to what it can do for them. It lurks like a potential stain on the reputation of the leader who believed that Workday would answer all their prayers with minimum maintenance.

In this chapter, we want to widen that perspective beyond HR and finance and to show that once this issue has been addressed through clarification of governance and shared support, the product can serve the best interests of the organisation as a whole. Leaders and their teams will come to learn that many of the solutions already lie in their own hands.

LIGHTBULB MOMENT

Our aim is to show you that, by using Workday effectively, instead of being driven by your business, you'll be the ones driving your business.

From day one, the SAHARA model will be the catalyst for transformation, leading to greater adoption, business alignment and valuable reporting. To understand how best to maximise those outcomes, it's important to begin by establishing some solid foundations. The first point is that you cannot achieve this by working in isolation.

Adopting good governance

need to understand

Most of an organisation's problems with Workday occur when governance is not established from the word go. Without clarity of governance, supporting the business proves difficult, if not impossible. If you're a leader reading this, the chances are that your department is shouldering most, if not all, of the responsibility in this post-Workday world. Your first port of call should be to involve other departmental heads because without collaborating with them, changing Workday will remain a mysterious and unwieldy task.

 LIGHTBULB MOMENT

Establish governance and let Workday do the rest.

As soon as the senior leadership team has made the decision to purchase and implement Workday, they need to start thinking about governance and what the team structure will look like. That means starting from scratch and deciding how they will support the key drivers behind everyday support queries, such as policies, passwords and processes. This immediately establishes a solid framework and provides a mechanism to begin

25

and manage the Workday journey. It also enables vital ongoing monitoring to look more deeply into the business and understand what internal issues are arising, where those issues are, when they occur and, most significantly, why they occurred in the first place.

A structure of support

Developing early knowledge of Workday in-house through your front-office support team, and facilitating insightful dialogue between business colleagues and departments to ask questions or seek enhancements, enables the smooth operation of Workday. Swift response to the business in those early days encourages greater user adoption. Frustration is easily preventable through the collaboration of HR, IT and finance support from the outset, because each will have identified whom to direct cases to.

A common Workday support model can be found at https://lightwork.global/lw247. A typical model has four tiers:

- **Tier 1:** Self-serve or chatbots using intelligent AI to assist business users

- **Tier 2**: Basic front-desk support resolving issues such as passwords and login problems

- **Tier 3**: Back-office support from HR, finance and IT to solve advanced Workday issues such as making changes to reports or amending a business process

- **Tier 4**: In-house experts on subject matter, or third-party input either from Workday or SI, to address complex advanced changes in Workday that require a business release in the form of a project launch

Of course, each organisation can employ its own specific support model within its industry. Our best advice is to identify at the beginning who the Workday Champions are in your organisation, and to collaborate directly with nominated individuals. This immediately frees up resources to work on issues as they arise, from the basic to the more complex cases.

When support teams have clarity about their accountability and responsibilities, nobody is left scratching their head and asking, 'Is this my issue to solve, or theirs?' And the end-user experience is dramatically improved. Nothing is more frustrating than when a simple issue isn't dealt with because it's not clear who needs to do what. Establishing good structure, with accountability and responsibility, leads to issues being resolved faster.

It's a common mistake to believe that because Workday is software-driven it's solely an IT concern when problems arise. An established collaborative governance structure solves that misconception because often the root cause and solution lie within HR and finance. It's vital for organisations of any size to assign leads to co-parent and support the Workday baby by bringing their specialist knowledge and experience to the table. This is the foundation on which Tiers 2 and 3 stand.

In Tier 2 support, assuming governance has been correctly established, business process owners can make full use of Workday's functionality and flexibility. This is the stage when advanced changes may be needed to the Workday business process framework itself. Of course, this happens during every implementation in every type of organisation; you just need to tweak and adjust business processes that will work for you. Sometimes those changes can be simple security adjustments that back-office support teams can make to benefit the business. More advanced changes, such as configuration, rely on advanced Workday skills which may be internally sourced or require external subject matter experts (SMEs).

Tier 3 is where complex changes are required. These may be impacted by external forces, such as changes in compliance and regulations including when Workday's own biannual releases are introduced, and how they are recorded and implemented. Any such policy or procedural change needs to be adapted within Workday's standard functionality. This is the heavy lifting part, which is more about designing, building and testing the required changes. We will describe the intricacies of this in Part Two.

CASE STUDY: DID THEY ADOPT THE WRONG BABY?

We were asked to help a client whose honeymoon with Workday was well and truly over. They were struggling with post-implementation but hadn't any form of governance to serve and support across Tiers

1, 2 and 3. The sense of frustration about Workday within IT and across the business as a whole was reaching boiling point. The perception and the adoption of the product were completely at odds with each other. Even the simplest of problems, such as password changes, couldn't be responded to or effected in a timely manner and the client was in the throes of abandoning the Workday product. It took the smallest of changes to turn this around – establishing a 'change governance framework' and assigning support teams correctly. Over the next few weeks the adoption rate increased exponentially. The question every organisation needs to ask is: 'Where does support for Workday sit and who is accountable and responsible to administer it?'

The most common problem we find in organisations using Workday is that they haven't established the lines of collaboration and communication outlined in this chapter. Their disappointment flows from the fact they want to jump right into the Augment stage without setting down the foundations first. It sounds obvious, but sometimes we all miss what needs to be done in our eagerness to open the box and to get stuck in. The problem itself lies in that word – 'stuck' – which is where many eventually find themselves, especially if the business doesn't have the skilled resources to rapidly change. Many HR and finance teams feel they don't understand how the IT aspects of Workday work, and IT don't know that they need to support HR and finance in a more holistic manner than they currently do. Little wonder that the honeymoon period is over.

Understanding your tiered Workday support model, communicating well and reacting quickly to queries maintains service integrity and facilitates successful adoption of Workday in your business. In the next chapter, listen out for a consistent monthly 'drumbeat' that will help to keep everyone focused and listening in the darkness for the right direction.

3
Authority

M any users fall out of love with Workday
because of their excitement and impatience to adopt all of its functionality from day one, when it contains an almost infinite number of features. Having reached a point when they need to make changes – either as part of a backlog of changes or because they want to introduce new functionalities – they enter all their inputs and, low and behold, Workday not only doesn't deliver but seems to generate more problems than it solves. The reality is that the problems lie within the organisation itself, and not the software.

This second part of the SAHARA model focuses on authority as the point from which change can be effectively and properly managed, ensuring that the business can focus on those elements that will drive both outcomes and value. This centre for authority can be known as the change approval board (CAB), the global design authority (GDA) or change forums (CF), but the key element that underpins each is that governance structure at senior level, and collaborating with HR, IT and finance teams maintains control in Workday. It's that formal place where requests can be collated and changes approved. It's where the decisions about costs, outcomes and values are made which then feed into the rest of the SAHARA roadmap. To understand what's not working when this goes wrong, and why this adds to many leaders' frustration with Workday, we will explain the root cause of the problem and the simple solution that fixes it.

Losing focus

Once Workday goes live within an organisation, even the most seasoned and highly experienced leaders and teams can, and do, lose sight of the roadmap – especially, of course, if one hasn't been put in place. Intellectually, they know that they have at their disposal a whole range of useful and impactful business processes and efficiencies that they believe they've implemented via Workday, but what's lacking is any formal governance. They've lost sight of the control that binds the functional teams to offer new input and monthly reviews into any changes that are proposed or have already been implemented under their radar. Part of that stems from an incremental apathy towards attending those change sessions, because the perception is that it's 'Just another Workday meeting'. A team working in isolation without collaboration often loses some of its internal vitality and becomes worn down by the problems they encounter.

LIGHTBULB MOMENT

The reality is that it's not a Workday issue, it's a people issue.

Without continual maintenance, the cultural map of the organisation becomes blurred, outcomes are skewed, and dysfunctional reports fail to reveal the whole story. With authority as a key anchor, and where a formal space exists to discuss and approve (or not) changes to the Workday function-ality as defined for the business, it is possible to manage and maintain the outcomes and to incorporate the biannual Workday releases. Getting that right from the beginning can make a huge difference to a business.

CASE STUDY: SPEND, SPEND, SPEND!

When we learned that a financial services client had spent £37m with two global SI consultancies, we knew there had to be a deep-seated problem within that organisation. They needed to implement new compliance and regulatory procedures. Had governance been in place, the solution would have been Workday and the cost would have been £2m. The key factor behind their decision lay in the fact that they hadn't organised a formal change forum. Had their IT people been involved in the Workday design authority, it would have been immediately obvious that the necessary change could have been implemented in Workday. The organisation felt it needed to fix the regulation updates outside of Workday at vast cost, but that wasn't the case.

It's vital that any organisation fully under-stands the power of Workday and what it's capable of. The business landscape is continually evolving, and Workday has been designed with that at its heart. Its functionality can answer all the relevant questions a business asks of it, but that relies on those responsible for the GDA being aware of all the changes occurring within the business and making sure that the harmony of those processes within Workday remain in sync.

 LIGHTBULB MOMENT

It's essential for any GDA to include HR, IT and finance.

Assigning in-house roles

Significant Workday changes, whether to process, data or security, must be owned and approved by leadership teams. That begins with assigning named senior individuals who are responsible and accountable for bringing requests for change to the senior leadership via the GDA. Without leadership driving these changes, it's little wonder that many organisations feel they're not seeing a meaningful ROI from Workday.

The HR, IT and finance teams need to fully adopt Workday and then assign an internal global and local business processor. One of Workday's most extensive areas is the management of absence (holidays, special leave, sickness etc), which is covered by almost forty separate business processes. With that inbuilt capability, why would any organisation hire a costly SI partner to manage their own absence processes? The answer is that they have not assigned roles in-house, and there is a lack of governance, which means no authority to manage change.

LIGHTBULB MOMENT

Establishing local and global business process owners is essential.

Owners that know the entire business landscape will understand each country's requirements under legislation and therefore how to present change. Locally, the change owner will establish regular and open lines of communication with the global process owner. In this way, control is maintained, which ensures that the owner prioritises the changes that the leadership and the business needs them to work on most. Changes are then fed into the strategic roadmap to ensure continual alignment. Those teams in organisations who best maximise their return are those who invest in people to effectively push efficiencies and processes throughout their business. They don't focus on their own needs alone, they prioritise what the business needs and how they, as a business service, can effectively serve it best for the benefit of all. As the business transitions through implementation, teams experience a rapid rise in knowledge transfer in their understanding of Workday. Ideas and suggestions will come from the business directly and go on a backlog for final presentation to the senior change board.

LIGHTBULB MOMENT

Avoid at all costs the temptation to implement every suggestion or change at once in the early days.

In Part Two, we describe in greater detail the pitfalls a lack of governance and structure creates. The key takeaway is to create internal team ownership to focus on alignment, correct timing of change, priorities, budgets, and deliver business outcomes, or ROI. The secret ingredient to success is to use the SAHARA model to establish a successful template for governance and structure around the business and Workday. This includes a monthly multi-departmental collaborative meeting where proposed changes can be presented to the GDA in a constructive way that focuses on business outcomes. The change request is presented by the named global business process owner and Workday change ambassador. More information can be found on the Lightwork website for governance and GDA via our Lightwork templates https://lightwork.global/lw247.

We know from our own hard-earned experience as Workday troubleshooters that when businesses fail to establish a formal GDA structure post-implementation, the lack of control leads to a mounting series of problems, not caused by Workday itself, but by people. In two previous instances (in the aerospace and insurance sectors), both sets of HR, finance and IT teams were initially enthused by the potential of Workday and its early adoption was extremely positive. Both businesses made the classic mistake of working through their backlog items tactically and embarking on a wide-ranging change initiative outside of any formal GDA structure. As a result, both experienced the same two impacts:

- The intensity, speed and volume of changes broke Workday with too much change too quickly, and didn't allow it enough time to 'embed' within the business.

- The leadership lost control of these changes and were annoyed that the business change priorities hadn't been set and agreed, which led to change that was not a priority in terms of helping the business.

This demonstrates the dangers of misalignment between the operational and the leadership teams, which occurs when control is not maintained within a formal GDA structure. Add to that the process of reversing those thousands of transactional changes and returning them to the backlog, and the cost to those businesses was significant – measurable not only in financial terms, but in time, energy and frustration for both the support team and the business.

Authority and a formal approval process are essential to fully implement changes based on business outcomes and a ROI for the change, whereas tactical changes implemented outside of an agreed governance structure lead to misaligned outcomes that fail to serve the business. This then leads to Workday user adoption fatigue and a system that is perceived to perform poorly, when in fact, it's a people issue.

Establishing a formal GDA structure creates a culture of Workday adoption and maintains control within Workday, ensuring business objective alignment: HR, IT and finance are the SMEs in Workday business processes, aligned fully to the business requirements and outcomes. Once the GDA is established in your business, create a pool of change champions which then widens the scope of issues that Workday can solve.

4
Health

Operating inside a Workday desert can feel hostile. It's also unhealthy because without a map or framework to follow, the oasis we have described can feel like a distant and unreachable goal and it's all too tempting to give up, give in to the inevitable and accept failure – but it needn't be like this. Health is vital, and our model will give you the head start you need to survive and equip yourself with the essentials to help you navigate your way through the complex pathway ahead. Clarity and not confusion sets in, and the route towards success reveals a clear and focused outcome.

Imagine you've just purchased a high-performance car. For the first few weeks it's a brilliant novelty, inbuilt with a wide range of high-tech features that set it apart from any other vehicle on the road, turning heads as you forge ahead in the fast lane, taking you autonomously from A to B with effortless power, with you in the driving seat having programmed in the destination coordinates. Just as with any car, irrespective of its premium price and high-spec construction, it still needs to be maintained on a regular basis to ensure its healthy operation. Some elements of maintenance are easy, such as cleaning the windscreen, changing the screen wash and filling the fuel tank, but if you ignore *any* of the basic maintenance its tyres will become worn and the vehicle unroadworthy, its untended spark plugs will misfire and the car will feel jittery, fail to accelerate or even start up. It soon loses its rhythm, and you lose trust in its ability to perform as you'd expected. Your high hopes have been dashed and you're constantly anxious about the impending breakdown.

Maintenance

Much of the car's magic, those elements designed to run seamlessly in the background, require an engineer's expert attention, and the same principles apply to Workday. When left unattended, Workday won't be able to look after your data, creating backlogs and incorrect positional reporting which could make you noncompliant with the regulatory bodies your organisation is governed by and subject to large fines. Without the necessary and ongoing checks in place, the faith that people initially had in Workday's business processes, data, security reports and integrations fades, and they feel disconnected from the outcomes. After roughly six months of Workday being left to run on its own, it starts to shake and stumble; people begin to feel nervous and point the finger of blame towards Workday underperforming. Populated as it is with thousands of daily transactions from across the whole business, Workday requires rigorous health checks to ensure its wellbeing, to keep it a clean and safe space and to sustain accuracy of data quality. Only then can it drive business decisions and outcomes for both managers and employees.

Nowhere is this more essential than in its security. This is not the exclusive reserve of the top-line InfoSec areas, where financial and regulatory auditors love to dig deep, but of those areas that are often overlooked – for example, when personnel exit the business, their access must be switched off immediately. The need to maintain that basic level of housekeeping for user access is of paramount importance and should be at the forefront of people's minds. It's too easy to lose control of basic, general reporting, forming a backlog which then needs to be corrected and leading to an unnecessary waste of time, energy and resources. Tying these processes to our SAHARA methodology ensures that all necessary features are aligned to the business, error logs are efficient and system protocols perform in the way that they were designed to, making Workday the upholder of your business integrity.

By ensuring that its organisations and reports are aligned, reviewing regularly and making business processes consistent and relevant, Workday facilitates various simple and intuitive auditing and monitoring features that many organisations allow to fall below their radar. When correctly implemented, these features are designed to automatically flag up any issues of concern as they arise – for example, when multiple and unauthorised personnel access sensitive data areas it upsets the rhythm of the business. Maintaining the health of Workday regularly as a standard symbiotic practice regulates these anomalies and prevents discrepancies in key areas such as:

- Data integrity
- Security
- Reporting
- Integrations
- Business process

Equilibrium

We will explain in more detail in Part Two the principles that we've identified to better monitor many of the issues we've highlighted in this chapter, and to achieve equilibrium, consistency and sustainability while operating within our SAHARA methodology. For now, the key questions leaders need to continually ask themselves are:

- How often do I collaborate with the leaders of other departments to ensure that my data, security, business process, integrations and reporting are implemented in ways that ensure

Workday is optimised to drive business outcomes?

- Do I run regular Workday health checks?

- Do I accurately audit and monitor reports to standards that meet external audit scrutiny?

- Am I letting things slide?

When the answer to the last question is yes, we find that clients have already fallen out of love with Workday. With no sense of direction pointing them forwards, their frustration surfaces because the data generated by Workday just doesn't feel right. The 'simple' reason is that they've failed to maintain its health. Just like the high-performance car, without the care and attention it needs, it no longer runs as smoothly and seamlessly as it did on day one.

When Workday health is maintained, it has the power to fundamentally transform every organisation it sits within and become the 'one source of the truth' that will tell you everything about your business and its employees. Workday is designed to deliver your ROI effectively and efficiently to maintain compliance at all times, but it will only ever be as good as the people and systems in place that keep it healthy. When implemented correctly, its inbuilt processes tell leaders if the data generated around security, integrations, reporting and workflows are in rhythm with the business and if they're all fit for purpose.

The top-line areas that typically generate significant levels of transactional data that leaders need to remain vigilant over include:

- **Legal regulation and compliance** – managing and deleting historical data in a timely manner and in accordance with data protection and privacy laws

- **Senior managers and certification regime** – regulatory requirements ensuring that senior leadership data is accurate, fit for purpose and scrutiny

- **Candidate data in recruitment cycles** – the permission you need from candidates to hold data over time

- **Job family framework** – job family groups, job profiles and grades normally linked externally, salary information for jobs

- **Missing data** – in key areas such as performance reviews, ratings or 360-degree feedback, manager records of one-to-ones

This may seem like an obvious list of priorities, but many leaders will never have considered carrying out a health check to understand the current status of Workday.

If you didn't do so when we mentioned it in chapter 1, now is an opportune moment for you to complete our Lightwork Thriving on Workday Quiz because this may flag up areas that need urgent attention, especially where you suspect the business is at risk of falling behind on regulation and compliance. Don't worry if you don't achieve a perfect score. Once you've completed it, you'll have the opportunity to access a set of health checks and compliance reports that Lightwork Global has built to assist in the highlighted areas that require attention. You can explore these at https://lightwork.global/lw247.

If regular health checks are not carried out, then Workday quickly falls out of sync with your day-to-day operations, and this leads to compliance issues, spurious data and incorrect reports. Interpreting any inaccurate data has the potential to misinform leadership decision-making and create a vicious cycle that points the finger of blame at Workday and not at the people entrusted with its maintenance. Trust is lost and Workday is seen as ineffective and producing irrelevant data. This is costly to resolve, especially when outsourced to a third party.

Our health check is the axis around which the model revolves, ensuring Workday remains aligned with the business. Fundamental issues can be fixed at source if you adhere to a healthy maintenance programme, and this can then lead to significant savings; for example, by averting inefficiencies that result in poor or missing data, or security breaches that are often not caught until the post-event external auditing process, resulting in eye-watering penalties levied by regulatory authorities. No business needs this from a financial point of view and it certainly doesn't need it from a reputational one.

5
Analytics

In the 'old days', how often would a C-suite leader ask, for example, HR to report what their current employee count was, only to be told, 'I'll get back to you with that in a couple of days'? Gathering any such complex data was time-consuming and no easy task. The one thing that could be guaranteed was that as soon as that figure was arrived at and presented, it would already be inaccurate, even if by the smallest of margins. Workday helped change all that and today that same request can be called up and seen in real time on a dashboard. No wonder C-suites, on learning this, exclaim, 'I want it. Buy Workday!'

Having data such as this at your fingertips is incredibly powerful and its value to businesses around the world, no matter how large or small, cannot be underestimated. Highly prized in all forms, it is rightly regarded as the new oil of the twenty-first century. Extracting every last drop of business data value not only offers organisations the opportunity to gain a complete, 360-degree perspective of how they are meeting their KPIs and objectives, it also allows them to measure themselves against the competition and gain the advantage.

Workday's inbuilt functionality and optional high-performance add-ons drill down deep to pump out data and are the main attractors that influence leaders to adopt and gain insights into its powerful capabilities. When the data-drilling parameters are correctly implemented, the analytics generated by Workday create a decision-ready organisation that fully utilises this data to improve performance and competitiveness. We've discovered that many organisations never realise the full potential of Analytics because they haven't formalised the processes as we outline in the SAHARA methodology.

Analytics will only ever provide meaningful insights and knowledge when the foundations of Serve have been established, Authority identified and adhered to, and when systems and processes are maintained via a continuous regime of health checks. Under these circumstances, Workday thrives as it's specifically designed to meet the business goals of data analytics by collecting raw company data and transforming that data into analysis to create insights that better inform strategic and operational efficiency.

The mistake we frequently encounter is that so many organisations believe that Workday reporting is an instant 'out-of-the-box' solution for every industry or sector, and as a result they struggle to maintain control of who is requesting and generating reports. They run into all manner of problems in interpreting the resultant analytics, which are often poor quality and present out-of-date or incorrect data. As the mountain of data grows, so the fear of tackling it grows and there is no clear line of sight as to how to stem the tide. It's no surprise when clients tell us that their greatest frustration with Workday lies principally in its apparent inefficiency in extracting meaningful data insights.

A new hub

We recommend that clients adopt what we call the Lightwork Reporting Hub – a central location where you can put all your reports and dashboards. It is the one location that leaders and managers can go to, knowing that the reports will be there. Those reports are then maintained through regular health checks to ensure that the data is monitored and the security accurate. Imagine the value of being able to call up real-time, instant and accurate data, on demand, that is strategically essential to the growth and sustainability of the business. Data is not to be feared when it's input correctly and extracted meaningfully. This is when the collaborations prescribed in the earlier stages of our model begin to shine and are recognised as central to the health and wellbeing of the whole organisation. At this point Workday powers into gear, relying as it does on a predetermined series of triggers authorised by the organisation to extract and enhance real data across the four fundamental areas.

1. **Descriptive** (What's happened?) – Identifying the precise number of absences in any given historical period, and which demographics have issues in the business.

2. **Diagnostic** (What's the effect?) – A summarisation of meaningful insights drawn from baseline data, such as varying compensation levels or diversity discrepancies.

3. **Predictive** (What's likely to happen?) – In-flight data that can flag up potential future employee attrition issues in specific departments or locations.

4. **Prescriptive** (How should we action going forward?) – Analyses employee trends and processes that can be adapted and tailored to align with the aims and objectives of the business, allowing it to plan ahead for likely eventualities, as opposed to reacting on the spot or standing still like rabbits in the headlights.

This sounds simple, and in essence it is. Your growing ability to navigate your path through the desert will lead to the oasis where the data mountain ahead is a gift, not a grind. Delineating your Analytics stage across the four areas outlined above will enable Workday to perform to its maximum capabilities and easily meet early expectations of extracting top-level executive data and generating business intelligence as the result of AI functionality. This enhanced capability helps businesses become more strategically aligned and, where necessary, more lean and agile operationally in areas that had once felt overwhelming and impenetrable as a result of basic reporting errors and misconfigurations.

LIGHTBULB MOMENT

Getting the basic reporting requirements right from day one is key to developing ROI and business buy-in though adoption with Workday.

Understanding those top-line operational and compliance reporting requirements, as seen through the lens of both current and historical data as it grows transactionally within Workday, is the foundation for establishing a firm analytical base camp to build on. The climb ahead will only be successful in reaching the summit if organisations ensure that their basic reporting systems are correctly defined and implemented. You can find out more about the hub on our website at https://lightwork.global/lw247.

CASE STUDIES: THE BENEFITS OF HAVING A DASHBOARD

Client 1

A finance company whose senior leadership team regularly needed monthly executive data analytics began to filter by key demographics, rather than just creating different reports. Lightwork developed a new dashboard called People Analytics inside the Reporting Hub and created filters. This allowed key business leaders to produce their reports in the way they wanted by selecting basic filters and reporting structures and data. These are now constantly maintained by the internal human resources information system team using the health checks.

Client 2

In an insurance company with a federated business model, each CEO required different types of reports based on specific insurance sectors, with one instance or source of truth being Workday. Using Workday's amazing security features and Report Hub, each insurance sector only had access to the reports specific to their own sector, all controlled, audited and monitored by one top-level Lightwork dashboard and controlled by one centralised team.

Client 3

A private equity client, with more than 1,000 reports, admitted to having lost control. The cost of testing all these reports during Workday upgrades was a serious pressure on time and resources. Lightwork helped the client introduce Report Hub and reduce redundant reporting. Today, after the health checks, only thirty reports and dashboards exist for the business.

These improvements are made possible via our 3A Blueprint, which requires organisations to invest in an SME in Workday reporting within the organisation. This is the key differentiator between chaotic and organised reporting, underpinned by the authority.

Accurate reporting

Too many organisations are tempted to skip this vital step in the process because Workday includes a simple report writer tool, but this is only effective when the business invests in training people to understand the base data objects that construct simple reports. Once that's a given, this control mechanism is the conduit to feed the essential analytics the business demands to move forward in a strategic direction.

We cannot emphasise enough the futility and waste of money that tactically generated reporting can cause over time, inevitably leading to error reporting, backlogs of densely packed, meaningless data, and costly solutions before leaders have even begun to contemplate climbing that mountain. With a governance model in place, every business has the ability to reach base camp, which is where most of the out-of-the-box compliance and regulation reports sit. These can then be related to basic areas of employee and company issues that leaders can tailor according to their industry. Even though they're basic, it is important to regulate and keep these reports compliant, as they are the necessary groundwork for any organisation progressing towards the more involved support offered by Tiers 2 and 3 that we described in Chapter 3. That's when organisations can begin to deep dive inside Workday to draw down on all transactional information and combine it with other business data that in turn opens seams of valuable insights into performance and competitiveness.

Visualising a mountain of data is one thing, but by thinking about climbing up that mountain from the base, step by step, organisations can drive insights and business decisions to executives. The perspective needs to shift, otherwise the view from the mountaintop risks being shrouded in fog, which isn't a good viewpoint from which to survey the landscape or spot the competition.

6

Return On Investment

Have you noticed that your colleagues have short memories? By that, we mean they don't always remember your hard-won achievements, but are focused instead on what's happening right now. They want to know how much value your department is delivering to the business by implementing the major changes you've initiated, and now you're on the back foot, chasing reports to justify your decision-making process. If that seems like a familiar scenario, it's our best guess that this is one of the principal attractors for buying into Workday: its capabilities are designed to give you that instant heads up, just when it's needed.

The problem is, without the foundations of our SAHARA roadmap in place, you find yourself running out of patience because Workday doesn't seem to be living up to its expectations. Now the bigger problem is that all executive eyes are on you, and somehow you need to justify the cost of the subscription level you originally encouraged the business to invest in. Despite a promising start, Workday seems to be little more than another piece of expensive underperforming software that won't deliver any meaningful ROI.

to avoid

ROI is the value created which enables a business to accelerate continual improvement faster and more accurately than had previously been possible, as a result of 360-degree thinking that connects all aspects of the business at a deeper level. Typically seen as a return over several years based on an initial capital investment for Workday, it's that revelatory point when it becomes apparent that Workday isn't simply an HR or finance system. Having engaged with our roadmap so far, hopefully your curiosity and expectations are on the rise again. We're about to explain that, when implemented using the foundational framework we suggest, ROI is not simply to be viewed in monetary terms but is best seen from a wider, integrated perspective.

 LIGHTBULB MOMENT

Workday is a value-generating powerhouse whose systemised implementation impacts on the entire cultural landscape and vision of the business. Talent is attracted and retained, inclusivity and diversity championed, and compliance and regulation maintained.

If that sounds warm and fuzzy, that's our intention. We want to show you that, when viewed from this angle, Workday can – and does – deliver way beyond its functionality. It creates and builds value not just in the moment and on demand, but also as a legacy reminder that you've been a crucial element in helping to shape and drive the strategic direction of the business.

A record of improvement

If you follow our SAHARA roadmap in the methodical order we present it, Workday will create an historic record of any improvement that's made via its implementation and any ROI is captured and assessed going forward. That may range anywhere from the impact of changes within the culture of the company, the talent, time and cost savings, through to any increase in revenue for the business. Workday captures it all – but it can't do this on its own, it needs the model to be in place for it to unleash its power through functionality. The ROI is becoming clear because Workday is working on the detail, the minutiae that remain invisible. Its data analytics capability is transformed from simple numbers on a spreadsheet to windows into the soul of the business, its culture and its people, revealing patterns and trends in behaviours and predicting outcomes as a direct consequence of strategic changes.

Following any change to Workday, ROI is automatically captured, from which point it's assessed continuously to ensure value exists and establish whether there are additional opportunities to create changes which will deliver additional value and ROI. Establishing authority from the beginning, then widening the group of people involved to push through changes, creates a vital and continual feedback loop. This is when iterative momentum, focused on business processes, gathers pace and shows in the minutest of detail the truth in the statement that the greatest asset of any business is its people, because they will be the ones driving the changes. That momentum sets the pace at which the business maximises the ROI through ongoing evaluation and review, challenging what's right for the business and where more efficiencies and synergies can be integrated within Workday to further enhance its value and ultimate ROI.

This is the acceleration path we confidently predict that businesses will begin to adopt, seeing Workday with renewed enthusiasm as they see their business change. The icing on the cake is that HR, finance and IT become an elevated, dependent and visible function that serves the leadership from the centre, in tandem with the intuitive Workday functionality that is designed to maximise ROI. Remember, its biannual releases are inbuilt to its subscription package specifically to update and introduce features that enhance its capabilities in response to clients' feedback and requirements. Every business benefits from its upgrades and additions via a pool of shared knowledge and continual improvement. These are proven key drivers in accelerating success and the releases are included as standard.

For the clients we consult with who have turned their attention away from Workday for all the reasons we've described so far, understanding how to implement the roadmap from start to finish is a game changer regarding Workday's ROI potential. They begin to see that they can successfully navigate the desert they've found themselves in and they reposition their internal GPS compass to view the landscape ahead from a whole new perspective. They're fascinated by the realisation that they hadn't set their course ahead with enough planning and precision. In their eagerness to get Workday up and running, they soon found they were lost, having persuaded the business to commit to an expensive expedition going nowhere. Being able to understand how they reached that point has been key to our own learning of why teams stray from the path.

One of those reasons was that the Augment phase is little short of exhausting. Without watertight authority, the process is haphazard and mostly guesswork, kneejerk or over-intellectualised. This approach fails to keep pace with the generation of thousands of daily data transactions that feed into Workday that no one leadership team takes full responsibility for – because the authority hasn't been established. Nobody is examining deeply enough if proposed changes or upgrades fit with their organisation or if ROI is achievable.

The leaders that do comprehend Workday's full potential to deliver value are the ones that can face the executives and, with complete confidence, report significant cost savings and efficiencies as a result of correct implementation. They know – and can demonstrate with their legacy reporting – that the business is fully compliant and that it comprises a diverse workforce with a mindful cultural fit. It's worthwhile for any leader to reconnect with the fire that lit beneath them when they first became aware of Workday or saw it successfully implemented within another organisation.

Monetary value

The elephant in the room is, of course, the money. So far in this chapter, we've circled around the obvious monetary focus because we wanted to highlight the inherent value that Workday delivers, but it can't be avoided, especially as any changes also create costs. This causes friction and concern when Workday is perceived as not delivering on its promises and may be deemed costly to improve.

Returning to our original assertion that mostly it's a people problem, not a Workday one, we've discovered where this area of contention can be unravelled. Many clients fail to prioritise changes inside Workday correctly, only for leaders to then challenge them on which authority gave those changes the green light, and the decision to adopt it is reversed, costing time and more money. Often, this is because there's a lack of agreement over what the business focus for change should be in the year ahead, and again, this results in going back and forth, spending to change, spending to reverse. It might sound obvious, but that's not indicative of an organisation spending money wisely.

Turn that round, and now there's a business ensuring it's focused on its priorities for the next twelve months, ready to spot the desired outcomes and quick wins which are all within Workday's powerful functionality, and the upgrades that usually take less than a day to configure. The wins when they arise are significant, which begs the question: 'How should we measure the ROI?' Is it the cost of additional implementation and add-ons, or the cost of implementing successfully that delivers huge value across the entire business for years to come, developing a twenty-first century, software-driven organisation that millennials want to work for?

It's no surprise that the 'FANGs' (Facebook, Amazon, Netflix, Google) are all using Workday to manage their greatest asset: people.

And Walmart

CASE STUDY: AN INTERNATIONAL INVESTMENT CLIENT

The business centred around soliciting 360-degree feedback from its key revenue driving personnel, who formed the backbone of the business and who the leadership was protective of. The leadership wanted to ensure that Workday delivered the best user experience from the outset and so we ran through the SAHARA model first and then implemented a 360-degree configured feedback solution that wasn't available in the out-of-the-box original version of Workday. As it happened, during this process, Workday then released a new 'anytime feedback' functionality which seemed to fit the client's requirement. To ensure that this would be appropriate, we took them back through the Authority stage and evaluated the potential solution versus the potential ROI and finally questioned whether this was the best route. The result was a far simpler process and a much better fit for the business. We viewed the problem and solution from a 360-degree perspective which the C-suite immediately took on board, ready for adoption. Thanks to the effective and dynamic simplicity of the upgrade, the eventual implementation only took two days to implement, creating a significant cost-saving benefit to the business.

Valuing people as well as ROI provides visible and tangible proof for senior leadership that Workday is worth the money, and that they have been central in maximising its potential to become a universal tool that helps accelerate the business towards gaining competitive advantage. It propels HR and finance from being a cost centre into a business and revenue driver. This is particularly noticeable when the adoption levels among the younger workforce increase because its functionality mirrors their user experience of social media and twenty-first century platforms when augmented correctly.

Perhaps by now you're thinking that it's time to re-evaluate Workday's ROI in your own organisation. Knowing where to begin has been one of the biggest challenges for Workday customers. Take a look at the Lightwork Target Operating Model (LTOM) on the portal at https://lightwork.global/lw247. This will help you begin thinking about the employee lifecycle in your organisation and the potential big savings in time and money that Workday can bring to your business if you invest in and track the ROI.

7
Accelerate

The final element of the SAHARA frame-work in this Amplify phase facilitates acceleration. Those businesses that engage fully with the Lightwork Amplify model see a direct correlation in the results gained from the Augment and Analytics phases as they begin to drive up the value chain and achieve more positive outcomes. Laying down the SAHARA foundations in Amplify is key to creating the springboard from which to implement Augment and Analytics in more powerful and meaningful ways – not only from within, by learning more about the employees and vice versa, but also from the external perspective of understanding the market. This is what we mean by engaging with Workday on a holistic level, on a journey that includes all the constituent and important areas – from governance, accountability, reporting, analytics, talent, performance, recruitment and retention, absenteeism, compensation, trends and behaviours, right through to the wider market landscape.

Seven top tips

1. Don't underestimate the power of Workday and use the inbuilt Adoption Planning features to drive an agreed roadmap for change.

2. Appreciate that Workday can be *the* gold source for company business data.

3. Don't ignore the significant ROI benefits post-implementation. Understand the benefits of each Workday release.

4. Access the mountains of untapped data more deeply because this provides huge business value.

5. Establish core internal global business process owners and report writing, hone skills and ensure proper governance to maximise business outcomes.

6. Maximise the leverage with Workday and SI relationships – these are two of the most underused assets and are always available to help.

7. Explore all the options available to minimise costs and implementation timescales of new Workday solutions so that they align to, and deliver more quickly, objectives and key results.

Where there are gaps in the functionality to be filled via additional configurations, the business will have a far greater understanding of Workday's capabilities, compatibilities and potential that will ultimately deliver its ROI. Any HR or finance team that is at the forefront of that level of insight, transforming it into a greater asset of incomparable value than ever before, will be viewed by the business leadership team in a different way.

HR and finance are seen together as a living, breathing business entity by the leadership, who will want to explore further anything they can do for the business beyond its traditional silo. By implementing SAHARA, business leaders with internal Workday SMEs will outperform their peers, including those within large multinationals who have budgets to match.

Now you've fallen back in love with Workday and have reconnected with the excitement you felt when you first encountered it, you're ready to move into Part Two: Augment, where you will see your renewed passion start to bear fruit with additional business digital transformation.

PART TWO

AUGMENT

Over the last ten years, Workday clients from around the world have generously shared with our teams their own ups and downs on learning to deliver successful large business change with Workday. The assets created in our award-winning hybrid Workday change implementation method – the Lightwork Precision Outcomes Wrapper (POW), built to complement Workday's own proven methods – have been specifically selected to cover problematic areas that are not always visible to business teams during large changes.

Our primary goal is simple: to enlighten our customers by passing our knowledge and experience on to them, helping them to avoid making costly mistakes and empowering them to sustain a truly digital transformation which elevates them and their internal teams in the eyes of the senior leadership.

Before we dive into the details, we'd like to share a few tips drawn from one-to-one discussions with our clients.

- You don't need expensive SI partners to deliver great change with Workday. Once confidence and knowledge are shared internally, the magic builds and gathers unstoppable momentum. At Lightwork we have witnessed this first hand many times because we made it a fundamental delivery asset to build knowledge transfer throughout the entire journey.

- Project cost and timelines surrounding the business change can be reduced significantly if you select the correct Workday delivery model (WDM) for your individual company, rather than basing this purely on the number of employees in your business.

- Being commercially savvy is key to unravelling as many benefits with Workday as possible and accelerating the ROI.

- Internal Workday Champions or Ambassadors drive and sponsor the success of Workday in companies that achieve greater change and business user adoption.

- Your TOM – and therefore the people and culture of your business – is front and centre of every step in the change.

- Being brave, bold and different is a recurring trait in those Workday clients who optimise and accelerate business change. They never stop thinking of ways to keep pushing the boundaries.

In the chapters ahead, we will explain how to simplify the approach to large change with Workday, raise the bar to focus on customer ownership and control, track business outcomes and switch the mindset away from the standard WDM delivered by the SI partner towards a more business-oriented delivery model – the POW.

The following diagram simplifies the wrapper by introducing it as two distinct layers – like peeling an onion. The inner layer contains Workday, Landscape and Environment, and

People and Culture; the outer layer contains Vision, Team, Commercials, and Control.

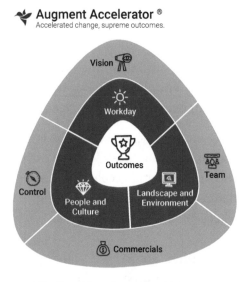

The Precision Outcomes Wrapper

Delivering major Workday change requires an overall view to match and track business outcomes for people, culture and process, and to link with other internal IT landscapes. Combining all these segments cohesively into a delivery mixing bowl is the secret to unravelling successful business expectations.

8
Workday Delivery Model

Organisations of all sizes are attracted to and buy Workday for many reasons, but principally because it's a one-stop software-as-a-service product that promises to seamlessly integrate a variety of core internal functions. Its advanced capabilities enable companies to adopt major changes which will affect the end business users by introducing consistent workflows.

The point at which difficulties can set in is during the implementation stage or when adding new features to increase business efficiencies and deliver a one-stop user experience.

The crux of the issue lies in knowing how to fully integrate and implement greater business functionality: in advanced compensation, expenses, payroll or learning management systems, and right across the spectrum where HR, finance and IT intersect with the business as a service. When less time is spent with the SI partner hand-holding the client, when the SI/ customer delivery experience is split 20/80, the client feels informed enough to think about the outcomes they're aiming for, and Workday no longer seems resource-hungry, time-consuming and costly.

Our aim is to help clients build on the insights they gained in the greenfield implementation phase so they can then raise the bar themselves and augment more effectively, resulting in them being more in control of real business outcomes and ROI. When the SI/ customer delivery experience is split 20/80, and the organisation is driving change to deliver functionality best suited to its business needs, it becomes clearer how Workday can transform processes and which additional priority enhancements are required to achieve new or improved long-term business savings or increased efficiencies. Depending on the size of the organisation, it will take anything

WDM

from three to twelve months for any larger elements of functionality to become fully embedded, and those may also need an additional Workday subscription and a dedicated and skilled internal Workday project team, as well as the SI partner.

The five key stages of WDM are:

1. Planning

2. Design and Architecture

3. Configure and Prototyping

4. Test

5. Deploy and Change

Imagine the WDM as a cake. Our approach adds 'outcome candles' that sit on the top of the cake across these five key stages of delivery to drive client-based awareness, understanding and confidence to meet the desired outcomes for the business. We act as 'gatekeepers' for success. The way we do this is by reminding clients that the pathway to major transformational change is easier to achieve when they use Workday's Enterprise or Launch methodologies.

Enterprise and Launch

Few leaders realise that there are two tried-and-tested delivery methodologies which are available at the beginning of every large transformational change:

- **Enterprise** – appropriate for large global companies with complex human capital management (HCM) or finance landscapes that are typically implemented by large worldwide SI partners

- **Launch** – suitable for medium-sized global companies with less than 5,000 employees, typically delivered by Workday or smaller SI partners in an out-of-the-box-style delivery, and utilises the hundreds of standardised Workday business processes with assumed limited configuration

Workday select's the method to be allocated to the organisation typically based on the size of the business (employee count). In some instances, this means a medium-sized global organisation given the Launch method could have benefited from the detailed focus on complex local requirements offered in Enterprise, as it best fits their own specific business needs, if they find they are struggling to adopt the Launch methodology.

The good news is you can elect which methodology to be allocated to your business according to your Design and Architecture stage, which considers whether it's possible to globalise in terms of standard business processes throughout the global business landscape without too many local country configurations, ie with HCM absence. The key difference in both WDM methods is your capability to configure localisation specifically for complex organisations. Medium-sized global organisations can have as equally a complex landscape as any giant, and the Enterprise methodology might be more appropriate to fit its needs. Smaller organisations can select a premium fixed-price model at a competitive rate.

Before a business considers embarking on any Augment stage, it's vital to think about which delivery methodology is fit for purpose, especially the more complex the organisation is globally in terms of culture, regulations and compliance. Knowing that you can select the right option for your business is a game changer in how successful Augment will be and you'll discover, perhaps to your surprise, that Workday and your SI partner will be amenable to your request, pointing out the nuances which differentiate between the two and helping you decide which fits best with your organisation.

The key questions to ask at this stage are:

- How are we going to effectively deliver this change into the business?

- Do we have sufficient time and internal resources to allocate to the project?

- Do we want to shift the balance from 80/20 to 20/80 so that the SI partner is no longer holding our hands but supporting us as we take the lead?

Whichever option is selected, the leader needs to weigh up the pros and cons. For example, an on-demand, fixed, hourly-based cost model allows the business some breathing space to evaluate the methodology where necessary, and to pause implementation in the middle of the Design and Architecture stage should a showstopping issue arise. That decision is influenced by whether you are being charged on demand, when costs can be ring-fenced or paused, or on a fixed-price term in which the clock keeps ticking, regardless. Some organisations on fixed price will want to maximise the onsite support to expedite their change process and will work towards that timescale. Others use the leverage of a fixed price to ensure they stay on top of it and push through decisions and signoffs.

Knowing there is flexibility that can be tailored to individual needs within both methodologies can help turn any current disappointment with Workday into a positive outcome. It puts HR and finance in control, allows the SI to fit around the business and releases the tensions around getting that desired business outcome and ROI.

A hybrid model

Our solution has been to introduce a hybrid version of Enterprise and Launch which includes outcome-based success factors at each stage of Augment. Using our customer-driven delivery model, supported by the SI partner, allows the customer to pause, breathe and take on knowledge transfer. For example, if you're a medium-sized business with a tight budget leaning towards the Enterprise method, company size isn't really a barrier. Have a look at our website https://lightwork. global/lw247 to find out more.

:grey_question: LIGHTBULB MOMENT

It's tempting for HR and finance teams to fixate on the WDM methodology and lose sight of the end-to-end business requirements.

Many leaders fear asking what success will look like at the end of Augment for the business. In our experience, not challenging or pausing to reflect until it's too late is one of the major reasons why projects go off budget and clients fall out of love with Workday. The problem is further compounded by the need for additional resources and the expense incurred by correcting mistakes.

Take a step back and quiz SI partners about the overall delivery and what success looks like after each stage of the WDM. Ask them to relay what has been designed and built for the business. The Lightwork hybrid model varies from the standard WDM in that we've created a bank of useful, additional assets that sit firmly on the customer's side of the delivery. These drive questions, checklists and time-outs back towards the SI and Workday, who can then track at each major stage that the proposed solution will be fit for purpose and achieve the desired business benefits.

CASE STUDIES: THE RIGHT MODEL(S) FOR THE BUSINESS

Client 1

One of our clients in the insurance industry recognised that they had selected the wrong implementation model for their own specific business needs far too late in the delivery stage, souring their colleagues' perceptions of Workday's capabilities. This resulted in a rapid fall in user adoption on deployment, as the end-to-end business workflow had not been fully captured at the Design and Architecture stage of the delivery. The Launch WDM had been selected without considering the client's overall cultural make-up – that it was a medium-sized organisation. Although it would have been better suited to the Enterprise WDM model, the client needed a hybrid of both delivery models to completely satisfy the complex configuration required in Workday.

Client 2

A multinational healthcare provider using the fixed-price Enterprise WDM model halted implementation six months in because it simply wasn't working the way they needed. They were at a standstill, with the SI scratching their heads trying to work on a new solution, while the clock was ticking like a taxi cab's metre stuck in a traffic jam. Halfway through the implementation, the client flipped from Enterprise into Launch – which at that time was the right delivery model – even though on paper they were an Enterprise-style customer. The Launch methodology was a much better fit all round for them in terms of their thinking, owning (20/80) and setting the pace of delivery.

Both stories are real examples of the tail wagging the dog. For the correct and most effective implementation of Workday, the client must be constantly asking questions, and not just accepting the answers as a matter of course. Our model sets out to avoid these costly, time-consuming and unnecessary pitfalls.

Try it for yourself – you only need to ask basic questions to open the conversation:

- What does good design look like for our organisation?

- How do I know that I've exited on a good design before I start to build?

- Have we designed the end-to-end business process outside of Workday that meets with HR, finance and IT service transition and operations?

- How do I know the SI has built a good prototype for me and that Workday is correctly configured for our organisation?

- Is the Launch or Enterprise WDM the right fit for our business, or would we benefit from a hybrid delivery model?

- What hybrid options are available, tailored to our specific needs, that are unique to our industry or business?

- What lessons learned from other Workday clients are available to avoid issues and guarantee delivering on time, to budget and to the desired quality and business outcomes?

- How do we avoid asking for more money from the business?

We've found that most unhappy Workday customers have tried to run before they can walk. Often, as the change sponsor – the person who is directing this major change and the one responsible for the quality assurance of the new Workday business solution – you will feel under pressure from the leadership to deliver tangible and total results as soon as the budget is allocated and the system goes live. We call this 'the Big Bang approach'. While this isn't a bad technique, the pressure and pace it demands often result in sponsors losing themselves in just the smallest implementations until they reach crisis point because nothing stands up. If they had been able to recalibrate the 80/20 rule in their favour, be more in control and not feel rushed into looking for perfection from day one, aiming instead for the ideal of continuous improvement with the SAHARA roadmap in place as the foundation for success, crisis could have been averted.

Now you're ready to put the foot on the gas pedal and accelerate towards faster, more efficient and quality solutions in the Augment stage. Everyone involved should know their responsibilities and accountability, as well as how to repeatedly change and test any future additions/modifications in Workday.

9

People And Culture

Almost all of our clients tell us that what attracts them most about their leadership role are the opportunities to interact with every element of the organisation, to help in their employees' development and to influence strategic business decisions. Their unique perspective into the business offers them a strong understanding of the organisation's priorities and challenges, but also enables them to influence the future of the company with the employment decisions they make. Why, then, do some feel that Workday isn't delivering the outcomes they want, despite its promised capabilities?

We're confident one of the answers to that is becoming clearer as you read this book: those leaders hadn't previously followed the SAHARA roadmap which underpins Augment. Other factors contributing to a lowering in the adoption rates of Workday are:

- The dependency on an SI partner to deliver solutions

- A decision-making process that is rushed and not given sufficient consideration

- The attempt to retrofit existing processes

- Losing sight of the end-users and the impact that changes will make directly on the day-to-day running of the business

The final point is perhaps where many of the issues arise during Augment. It's vital to ensure that the principal recipients of this change – people and culture – are at the heart of everything.

Design workshops

We recommend that when the change sponsor enters the design workshops they do so with firm views as to what their TOM will be for this particular change. That's not to suggest they won't be challenged by Workday or SI partners, who may have different ideas on how to implement the proposed changes. Nor are we saying that the change sponsor won't need to shift their thinking as they go through the process. What we are saying is: be prepared.

An SI might say what's being proposed isn't possible. On the other hand, they might present alternative ideas and solutions already built into Workday that the change sponsor hadn't been aware of. An idea could be raised by one of the internal SMEs whose insight into a particular process will be invaluable during the design workshops at the beginning of Augment.

It would also be beneficial for the change sponsor to approach the design workshops from a nontechnical point of view. Workday is a sophisticated, mind-boggling technology, which is why SIs and experts are on hand to help make the impossible possible.

 LIGHTBULB MOMENT

Just like getting on a plane, don't think about what makes Workday fly and stay up in the air, stay focused on the destination.

Think about what's right not just for today, but also for the future, because that might influence your thinking about how you implement this change. This is the point where you need control over the change timeline and the important business end-to-end process, so don't be tempted, or let anyone force you, to rush into it. Our mantra is 'Take your time', then you can have those conversations with the SI. A lack of space and time is one of the many perceived pressures of Workday, with clients believing they must go with the flow – Workday's flow. You can – and must – control that flow yourself during this crucial front-end Design and Architecture stage, especially if you're considering making big changes that will impact the whole organisation and affect how far you should push the game-changing self-service model which hadn't been an option until now. Perhaps you need to implement the centralised service model more because that's appropriate to the culture and make-up of your specific organisation.

 LIGHTBULB MOMENT

Our Lightwork hybrid model makes sure timeouts are provided to get the business design and outcomes end-to-end before moving on to build in Workday.

It's not Workday or the SI's responsibility to suggest which approach is right or wrong; that decision lies with you and your need to do what's right for your business. A small change, such as enabling employees to book their holiday periods themselves via Workday, and thereby handing them a level of personal control, can have a huge effect, which in turn leads to greater Workday adoption across the board.

The correct path for your business will depend entirely on its culture, where you want to take it in the future and how much autonomy you want to give your employees. These are all factors to consider when thinking about the bigger picture, what those processes will be, and which will be tied into the GDA that you helped establish in the Serve and Authority elements of the SAHARA roadmap.

The design workshop is all about you and your specific business needs. It's then that you can take the decisions and select the processes that are the best fit for your organisation culturally, as well as for the people using a process once it goes live. Workday already has the whole range of business processes built into it and ready to roll out and you could simply select the out-of-the-box deliverables recommended by your SI partner – but don't do this at the expense of first determining if they fit the bill.

If, like many, you feel bamboozled by the technical terminology, don't be frightened to ask your SI how everything connects, so you can understand the impacts across the wider Workday landscape – payroll, IT, talent management etc. Prior to any change going live, be 100% certain that you understand all the impacts of that change on the people and culture, and on any other business processes both internal and external to Workday.

CASE STUDY: A CENTRALISED MODEL FOR RECRUITMENT

One of our clients – a private investment entity – was thinking about following the trend to rush towards the employee self-service model and to devolve recruitment responsibility from HR, allowing managers to own the entire process. In the design workshops, when this was thought through in detail and the impacts assessed, it was decided that a centralised HR model for recruitment would be a better fit for their organisation and culture because their people were too busy earning money for the business without needing to take any additional

HR self-service responsibilities themselves. That was the right decision for this business, even though Workday provides a brilliant alternative solution. Had the client not thought through the self-service/centralised models at the Design and Architecture stage, they may have adopted a functionality at cross purposes with the business.

Big-picture thinking

When you're thinking through the business processes framework, don't get stuck in a silo mentality. You need to be constantly thinking about what's right for your people, culture and ROI within the whole landscape. A little bit of forward-thinking and knowing your prerequisites will help you to get the best outcomes from the overall Design and Architecture stages.

For example, when you're thinking about your recruitment and third-party agencies, ask IT if that means external third parties will be connected into your dataset for the first time, and if they are, is that an identity issue or a compliance problem? Do you need to involve your data protection people? (Absolutely!) It's the wider thinking that's vital at this People and Culture stage.

Be prepared, but be open to ideas from others, including the Workday SI partner but particularly from the SMEs and other organisations of a similar scope and size, of whom it's completely acceptable to ask for their best practice advice. As the change sponsor who is making fundamental decisions, it's OK to reach out.

Ask Workday, your SI or your SME if they know anybody in your industry that you can talk to. The answer will be that there's always someone, and often those discussions can offer a level of clarity which nobody else within your own organisation could. A change sponsor might think that a centralised model is the route to go, but the game can shift and, having talked to an industry peer, they decide to go self-service because they now see the bigger picture and benefits. If you are considering making a fundamental or radical change to a process, there's nothing to be afraid of in asking for a timeout to the workshops. There's no need to be railroaded into making a decision based on your SI's urgency to complete their delivery schedule. Don't rush, pause

where needed and design the system specific
to your business and future outcomes.

CASE STUDIES: IT'S OK TO PAUSE

Client 1

One client of ours, whose industry is regulated
by the Financial Conduct Authority, was
working on a learning project in the design
workshop and assumed mandatory learning
was an annual event. There was some doubt
and confusion within the team, and nobody
agreed on whether that was correct or not. It
was agreed to take a small break and pause the
design to seek expert external advice. It turned
out that the original assumption was incorrect.
Workday was configured to reflect mandatory
learning on a quarterly basis, which was the
right cultural fit and created the desired
outcomes for the business.

Client 2

During a second recruitment design workshop,
a client change sponsor asked us how far we
believed we were in the process. We estimated
that we were at almost 70% but that we
wanted to reach 80% fit for business purposes
(before prototype build). We took time out to
resolve a difficult integration issue, found a

reminds me
principle)
of
P. P proof of

solution during a mini discovery workshop and then tested it. We didn't complete the design until we had all decided which were the best outcomes for the business and then reached that 80% fit-for-purpose target for P1.

These examples prove the importance of approaching the design process with the concept of taking time out, as and when needed, built into it. Don't fear giving yourself that breathing space to consider the process properly, especially as all changes will impact on your people and culture. Misjudging this will cause unnecessary friction down the line and a rapid drop-off in Workday adoption rates. Don't be pressed into deciding, by the SI or anyone else, without giving your full attention as to whether your decision will be right for the business. An SI will be looking to tick their box of completed tasks so that they can move on to the configuring and prototyping of Workday. In many cases that's unlikely to provide a delivery and outcome that's right for your business. It will be second best.

By holding internal mini discovery workshops before you even start with your design workshops and agreeing internally what principles you will follow, you will uncover any gaps in your thinking across the entire organisation, which will prove invaluable should you find yourself in head-to-head arguments globally and locally around design.

Always include someone in your design workshops who focuses on people and culture. This is a good moment to assign a change sponsor or better still a Workday Ambassador who will eventually sit on the SAHARA Authority in Amplify. Timeouts allow you to consider in more detail how any change will impact your people and culture, and they can be a useful way to consult with industry peers and external experts.

Always consider your TOM and remember that the operating model can be fine-tuned or even changed completely. Senior business leaders must be aware of major changes early in the key Design and Architecture stage so these can be influenced and championed. In adopting our approach of considering your people and culture, you will build the best outcome for your business. Workday is the workhorse, the process is your blueprint, but the people and culture are the key to success.

10

Landscape And Environment

This chapter will help orientate you towards 'future-proofing' the Workday technical design (landscape) with your internal technical infrastructure teams (environment) and show you how to avoid some painful design decisions Lightwork has experienced first-hand. Before you let out a big sigh of, 'I don't do technical,' and move on to the next chapter, please allow us a few minutes to explore important high-level areas way beyond the Workday platform.

This topic is enormous, and we could dedicate another book to designing, building, deploying and supporting system integrations and other IT topology with Workday. All teams worldwide who develop and maintain Workday do a fantastic job. Delving deep into the Workday architecture and learning the heart of the technical product takes time, dedication and money from highly skilled personnel on a steep learning curve. The level of knowledge they acquire as the Workday products grow twice yearly is astounding.

Discovery sessions

Bad technical design ultimately damages linkage between Workday and other vital core systems, and it is at this point that we see senior leadership's buy-in with Workday start to fade, and that all-important ROI look less likely through increased technical costs. Many Workday customers find themselves learning the hard way when they are faced head-on with 'technical debt' that occurs for many years after implementation. Many see increased IT / application management services (AMS) costs year-on-year to support the current business infrastructure with Workday as the master data repository for *all* downstream business systems that need *live* people information.

Much focus is placed on technically ensuring payroll integration delivers consistent data accuracy due to the nature of paying people and legislation requirements in each country. Why, then, is the same emphasis and due diligence, care and attention not placed around other systems which, though slightly less critical, will ultimately affect Workday adoption and business decision-making processes if not accurately updated?

Throughout this book you have heard the drumbeat of our message in the areas of business vision, governance and team collaboration. These are the key ingredients that will help move your business towards successful technical outcomes. The Lightwork Landscape and Environments model asks our clients the following questions:

- Do the new business processes you have designed in Workday allow for data flows – both manual and automated – to fit with your current and future IT infrastructure technology?

- Are you integrating the best possible technology services, which are modern and easily supported for years to come by your own internal business support teams?

- If you want to 'swap out' a system connected with Workday in the future, has the integration you have developed been designed for simple disconnect, remap, transformation and import into your business-critical systems without needing external technical Workday resources creating new additional costs?

- How much technical debt are you going to carry at the end of the Workday implementation? What will your overall end-to-end solution look like inside the business technical framework in the years to come and do your internal resources understand the data flows, configuration and technical solution to the point they can support without external help?

- Have point-to-point connections either supplied by Workday out of the box or custom-developed by an external Workday

SI partner been thought carefully about in the design in terms of years of operation? Workday offers hundreds of connectors that are managed and maintained by both Workday and third parties without much knowledge or configuration needed to support them. Exception and error handling is important to maintain accurate and consistent data and is one of the chief reasons why Workday data falls out of sync with other vital data sources.

- Have you considered using a centralised data hub – a single bidirectional update from Workday to a data repository owned and managed internally – to feed *all* downstream systems?

Taking the time to answer these questions and others in discovery-style sessions and during the Workday Design and Architecture phase will pay incredible dividends in the future support of your business. Lowering IT costs via good design, appropriate automation and simple technical solutions leads to future-proofing or upstreaming for a challenging and constantly changing world.

CASE STUDY: A SUCCESSFUL PLAN B

In the middle of Workday HCM implementation in a large, London-based insurance company, Lightwork were called in by the chief people officer (CPO) to assist as the delivery was failing to complete on time and budget. After a review, Lightwork found the main culprit to be complex integrations, including payroll. The delivery team were down in the technical weeds, having lost their true focus on implementing Workday to the agreed timescale and budget in accordance with the signed-off business case.

The Design and Architecture phase of the implementation had identified the need and desire to develop thirty-five fully automated point-to-point integrations. Some of those integrations had less than ten transactions per month that could easily have been managed manually or delivered using a simple data report from Workday, imported monthly and allowing the implementation to remain on time and budget. The payroll integration was equally complicated by trying to fully automate when this payroll product was not best suited to the Workday data architecture. Lightwork initiated a plan B for this client to successfully deliver Workday to the agreed business case, which the payroll integration and others developed and tested using a combination of Workday reporting and manual intervention.

After successfully delivering Workday, the client did end up having a walk in the desert and then in the wilderness, having to manage for years the technical debt incurred by maintaining so many complex integrations. Many were customised and not the standard out-of-the-box types that Workday provides. External Workday SI support was needed to maintain the custom integrations that increased the overall operational challenge for HR. This was done via AMS – a contract taken out with an external Workday partner in the ecosystem, either at a fixed price or based upon a pre-agreed number of hours for upgrades and continuous improvements. Ultimately, this meant the executive board saw Workday as an expensive, high-maintenance product, which could have been easily avoided by asking the questions suggested above and taking a view to simplify the delivery and integration in the years ahead.

Before the Design and Architecture stage, Landscape and Environment is a key factor in the commercial negotiations. Our experience at Lightwork shows that not enough time is allocated to testing beyond Workday and this can lead to poor integrations with other systems that pull on IT support consistently and will, over time, affect the business users with incorrect or misaligned data in downstream core systems. Our POW concentrates on 'upstreaming the tech' at the crucial stage of Design and Architecture. During the design workshops for Workday, workflow concentrates on the configuration inside Workday. Other crucial business systems are often not discussed, and the end-to-end design is not covered and agreed upon. Taking the time to flow data fully through the design end-to-end helps whittle out any major concerns and builds overall knowledge transfer.

11

Commercials

Just as the technical delivery of Workday can be bamboozling for the uninitiated business leader, so too the associated commercials can appear daunting, with confusing legal terms, conditions and pages of jargon that outline accountability, responsibilities and costs. Statements of work (SOWs) are linked to overall master schedule agreements (MSAs), and other types of contractual and binding agreements can appear as a 'dark art' of business – only fully understood by procurement and legal teams.

Business leaders need time to stop and build a clear, commercial understanding and binding agreement directed at Workday and the SI partner, designed to guarantee successful business outcomes and, more importantly, establish which actions should be taken if those outcomes are not met by both suppliers. Commercial elements should be built into the SOW to form the binding agreements and joint accountability. Clear milestones and targets need to be set, and the implications discussed of those not being met by either the client or suppliers in relation to project timelines, budgets and the desired delivery assurance and business fit-for-purpose solution at the end of the project.

Significant consideration should be given to costs, which should be capped where possible if they unexpectedly increase due to timeouts required during design. This establishes the end-to-end process for the business, as well as the intention to get it right the first time around. Don't accept a second-rate solution that the end-users won't fully adopt, resulting in them starting out on the wrong foot.

The POW builds on the WDM and adds client-based models to focus on delivering a commercially viable solution that meets with the business outcomes. We suggest using the POW throughout the entire Augment process, allowing the business commercial change director time to consider a more rounded and trusted vision of the overall change, and commercially agreeing a 'blueprint for success' with everyone involved. Our suggestion may seem radical, but it will alter whether you run over time, budget or solution quality, and give you the full confidence of the sunny uplands ahead if you are commercially savvy.

Below are some key considerations. They are not beyond the thinking of most procurement departments, but they are in our experience important pointers to make sure you get the best commercial deal for your business.

Don't sign up immediately

Wow! We can almost feel 'the Eye of Workday', like Saruman from *The Lord of the Rings*, turning to look at us from Pleasanton, California. Give us a chance to explain.

In the context of how we have framed the customer/supplier relationship between the business needs, Workday and the SI, this is not such a ridiculous idea. Throughout this book we've been encouraging you to think about how your business change will begin and end by forming prerequisites, taking due diligence and timeouts, not getting starstruck with WDM models. We've encouraged you to think holistically about the business endgame; how to deliver truly good change for every employee, manager and senior leader to admire; and how to create that essential ROI for the business for years to come by delivering a programme of change on time, on budget and which hits the desired target dead centre.

Remember, as change sponsor only you understand your business as well as you do, so before you commit to any Workday licence agreement or MSA/SOW with an SI partner, make it a priority to ask for stage payments from your SI until you are completely happy with the overall Design and Architecture stage. This key stage needs to be fully developed and agreed end-to-end in the business, as it is the foundation of success. Visiting your SI too late in the delivery with a need to pause or change direction will hurt you and the business. We've seen this happen time and time again, even with the savviest change leaders, because they didn't realise that they could have thought earlier about the outcomes they desire, and that they could have briefed Workday or the SI to deliver success, either in the greenfield implementation or Augment stage.

LIGHTBULB MOMENT

Before committing funds to your change programme, request that Workday include training costs as part of the overall licence package.

The cost benefits in doing this will be significant, as the investment in assigning your teams to key roles such as the global and local process leaders, report writers and change champions inside the business means your organisation is ready to avoid the Desert and the Wilderness of the Lightwork 3A model and move from Postlaunch directly into Optimise, Transform and Thrive.

Workday are always open to negotiating options that will best suit your financial needs – so remember to discuss these with them. If you don't ask, you don't get. Even though this all revolves around technology-based deliveries, it's important to remember that the H in HCM refers to 'human'. That human-to-human interaction between client and supplier remains the initial key to achieving the overarching success of Augment, and money always talks – in business, it's often the major cause of misunderstandings, disputes or disappointment.

Workday is a premium enterprise product so naturally the bar is already set high, even for smaller clients that are willing and prepared to commit to the outlay on the licence itself. When you then factor in the costs of implementing changes in Augment with an SI partner, that's another layer of expense, even before the costs of your own team's input is included.

 LIGHTBULB MOMENT

Many Workday customers don't realise that once you've signed for a licence the costs begin immediately, regardless of a six- to nine-month delivery ahead.

Work with your team

A savvy procurement team is worth its weight in gold. These are the ones who love to strike a good deal and to negotiate with suppliers. The best teams we've seen haven't shied away from setting the terms of the Workday licence on a more favourable footing. We've seen some staggering results negotiated in advance. The standard Workday licence terms are based on the number of employees, but also rely on an annual incremental percentage increase. Sharp procurement teams have negotiated to ditch the incremental rise and replace it with an annual 1% fixed increase – resulting in a considerable saving to the business without any loss of quality provision.

Issue a statement of work

Remember that your business is the customer, and that must always be where the focus is aimed. It's your responsibility as the change sponsor to agree a solid statement of work with your SI partner, so be prepared to put the time and effort into understanding the needs of your environment, people and culture. The lesson we've learned from organisations with unsatisfactory outcomes is that there has been insufficient consideration before the programme began. We strongly recommend that the SOW clearly identifies the following:

- Who's doing what and when. A good plan on a page with timelines is essential.

- Who's accountable. Tables of major tasks should clearly detail who does what and in which order.

- Who's responsible. Routes of escalation need to be planned for the event of things going wrong, with an agreement on the quickest process to resolution.

- What success looks like at each delivery stage.

- How success is measured with customers and suppliers.

A solid SOW is indispensable because in the event of any slippage it serves as a reminder and record of what's been agreed with your SI partner. It puts your business at the centre because the agenda is set for the foreseeable future in complete alignment with your needs and on a strategic path that has been given all due care and attention from day one.

The danger is that the organisation agrees to move forward with the design in another classic example of the tail wagging the dog and rolls out the standard commercials to fund it, based solely on the SOW issued by their SI. The change director agrees this in the confidence that this is the right approach because it's the norm, but what they don't realise is that these SOWs are specifically designed from the supplier's perspective, not the customer's. Even if you've identified the need to implement an SOW or more significant changes, you can't expect an SI to do it all for you.

We can't emphasise enough that flipping the focus upfront so that it's 20/80 in favour of your business is how you will get the best from Workday and its SI partners.

CASE STUDY: BOXED IN

In the Launch methodology, one SI clearly stipulated that the commercials relating to the customer only ever allow it to change two business processes in recruitment, and that the others should all be out of the box because Launch is a fixed-price service. It's the customer, then, that's literally boxed in. Unless of course they've been savvy enough at the

> beginning to state they want more flexibility, as well as a greater understanding of what the SI is proposing.

Don't simply be led by Workday and your SI partner's first offer and proposed plan of action. Take your time, discover with your colleagues what you need to achieve and then build your commercials around those needs, making sure no stone has been left unturned. Then go back to Workday, because the minute you sign as a customer, you're paying the licence *from that day forward*. It often catches clients by surprise when they realise that they're paying for recruitment, or learning, long before they even implement it. Using your SOW to strike a good deal is far preferable to returning cap in hand to the leadership asking for a higher budget because something was missed earlier in the process.

Request milestone payments

A good negotiation will give your business the flexibility to hold back a meaningful percentage until the SI hits several milestones, as stated in the SOW. This then drives behaviours and incentivises the SI partner to bring everything that they've got to the table, and only when you're happy that they've delivered what you need will they invoice for the balance. This is not unusual practice, and you may be surprised how often clients and SI suppliers reach such an agreement.

Our model at Lightwork is based upon milestone outcome payments. It's a completely different mindset that allows our clients to be fully confident that they're receiving maximum value. This shift towards the customer is essential, especially for small and medium-sized business enterprises, so that they can engage and take advantage of the best that Workday can offer.

Continuously review

In adopting our Lightwork POW and allowing yourself more time to think in depth about WDM, People and Culture, Commercials, Landscape and Environment, Vision, Control and Teams, you focus on the primary objective: the business and its desired outcomes.

That can *and will* result in huge savings across the board. Take your time and ask yourself:

- Are we approaching this in the right way for our business by adopting a phased or Big Bang method?

- Could we delay costs with Workday until the design is complete?

- Would just-in-time training prepare us for better design workshops, so the team understands Workday and the terminology better, and lead to greater success?

- Have we agreed milestone payments with the suppliers who have skin in the game?

- What happens if the timeline, costs or delivery assurance start to slide?

If any issues of concern arise in the discovery and mini workshops, you've bought yourself the time to iron those problems out while saving a large part of the programme budget that could well be needed downstream on testing, deployment or change and communications. At Lightwork we call this 'upstream thinking'.

It's incumbent on advisory partners like us to recognise the need to change practice and perspectives so that the focus is on serving the customer. The traditional Workday methodology doesn't fully allow for that, and often it's when the commercials begin to run beyond their initial parameters that leaders fall out of love with the platform.

We want you to avoid finding yourself in that position by using the Lightwork POW as your guiding principle before you even commit to a single penny more than necessary. We know it works because we've tried and tested it successfully with clients over a twenty-week period. This involved two weeks of discovery and planning the commercials and design, and eighteen weeks implementing without any issues arising or any additional expenditure. We've proved that we can flip the Commercials stage on its head and tailor it more to the client's needs using the appropriate methodology.

As with anything in Workday, the commercials can serve you rather than the other way round if you approach them in the right way. This includes being more commercially savvy with Workday, the SIs, suppliers, third parties and internal divisions; programming prerequisites and discovery stages to be completed before signing up commercially with Workday; and not spending before you need to. Milestone payments built into delivery plans based on success criteria drive better behaviours and better-quality outcomes.

By being prepared in advance, by looking at the overall commercials from your own perspective first and in accordance with your needs, and with a little creative thinking and simple negotiation skills to back you up, there's no reason for the commercials to be the final barrier to entry, or the reason why you should fall out of love with Workday.

12
Vision, Control And Teams

It's such a simple word – 'vision' – and yet we all have our own interpretation of what the business vision, goals and objectives should be. We know that out-of-the-box business process frameworks and products have been delivered for many clients, but why is vision important for Workday?

Having a clear line of sight and overall strategy is essential to drive 'correct' change in your business. The ability to measure the success of change over time in terms of quality, costs, efficiencies, adoption and regulation should be at the forefront of your mind and on your continuous improvement map. Think of major change as two different sides of the same coin. One side is about implementing the change successfully in Workday, with all its nuances. The other is about the business and operational value which this change will bring, and that adds benefits, increases productivity or efficiencies and helps managers and employees with everyday tasks.

LIGHTBULB MOMENT

One size rarely 'fits' completely; some alteration is always required.

Organisations that make great changes and give executives, managers and employees meaningful Workday experiences have two things in common:

1. They plan and execute changes based on the priorities of the business or they focus on key initiatives that impact the business in the best possible way in terms of value, outcomes or ROI. These initiatives are captured using the Workday Adoption Planning and are driven by senior management and operational teams

through the GDA for acceptance, denial or parking. Only the top features make the grade to be taken forward and launched by the business.

2. They create and execute a TOM for HR and finance. Each year both functions take time out to poll and develop business initiatives. This is followed by a review of the corporate strategic direction from the executives based on the world today, market factors and specific events that relate to their own industry to drive a change path.

Many Workday clients dive headfirst into additional major changes without considering the overall vision of the business as a priority. We recommend a comprehensive business case for every major change with Workday. Many HR and finance teams struggle with writing compelling business cases to achieve additional funding. Workday has dedicated teams worldwide to help their customers. They are called the Workday Value Proposition team and they offer *free* services to help build business cases and roadmaps for customers.

LIGHTBULB MOMENT

A good business case not only outlines the key business benefits, costs, value and ROI, it leads to senior management awareness and acceptance through a jointly agreed and sustained vision for change.

One of the first areas to consider when thinking around change should be the biannual releases from Workday each year. If you select the right features to implement, these upgrades have the power to gather quick wins in your business. At Lightwork, we focus our clients on these releases and break down the features across finance and HCM, which then form part of the February and August change meetings, encouraging the global and local business process owners to present changes in major functional areas. Look at the following Lightwork diagram and ask yourself: 'In the last six years, how many new Workday features has my organisation adopted to improve the daily administration and tasks for every user in the business community?'

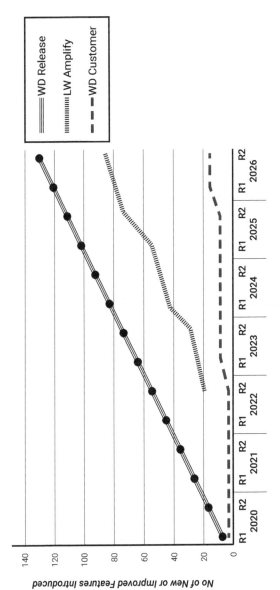

Workday Updates Over a Six-year Period

No of New or Improved Features Introduced

Legend:
WD Release
LW Amplify
WD Customer

Only around 20% of Workday customers are adopting new features across all releases and they tend to be the ones running fast on change, viewing the whole business from the top of the mountain and offering exceptional service and insights. These are the Workday customers at the vanguard of their industries.

Internal and external structure

To have that vision of overall change, the required governance we mentioned in Part One and the change roadmap, you will need to have a solid team of people dedicated to supporting Workday internally within your business. At the beginning, teams are forming, storming, norming and performing and this collaborative approach can be breathtaking to behold. Productivity, problem-solving and that all-important team spirit with internal and external suppliers just keeps on accelerating. Knowledge of Workday grows day by day. You witness individual brilliance along with the various teams' commitment and see people shining under pressure. You consider just how good it is to watch your own team growing, learning and developing new skills while delivering fast-paced change that is serving the organisation successfully. High hopes and big visions are born in this new digital experience and the desire to do more is openly evident.

LIGHTBULB MOMENT

The key to successful change is knowing 'how' to navigate and 'where' to go and most importantly 'when'. Begin to walk, then run to your desired destination with ability and confidence.

It's when those high-performing teams begin to disband, and your SI partner and skilled external resources leave for Workday projects with other customers, that we see common and fatal themes begin:

- Internal teams are exhausted from the high-pace project execution – normally having to manage day jobs in addition to playing a major role in the Workday delivery.

- Leadership often say they have 'Workday earworm' and want to focus their attention on other strategic initiatives in the immediate future.

- 'Change fatigue' is a term often heard through the business corridors.

- The sense of camaraderie is lost, replaced by the new sensation of being on your own without the support and knowledge of the project team. This begins to play on the internal team's mind, and a feeling of vulnerability and apprehension about the months ahead sets in. You've begun the long walk on your own through the blistering desert. You now find yourself on the wrong side of the Workday path.

In Part One we covered the importance of overall leadership and governance as well as controlling the flow of change. The key to success is establishing core internal teams that are accountable and responsible for optimising, developing and thriving on Workday. This is no different to landing large business transformations and adding major features like Workday Learning.

To gain a better understanding of what constitutes a successful team structure, and the role different people will play, review our example HCM functional team structure at https://lightwork.global/lw247. Each organisation will differ, but it's vital to understand the importance of assigning internal people to each role to build internal accountability and responsibility.

Top tips

- Internal people can be assigned to many functional roles depending on the size of the organisation. For Workday Launch and medium-sized Enterprise customers, this will always be the case.

- Lightwork encourages every Workday customer to assign a Workday Ambassador who is a senior leader within the organisation and sits with a Workday 'hat' on at major meetings.

- Invest in good leads for security, reporting, data and integrations. These people will pay dividends over and over again. As the business advances, so does the reliance on Workday becoming a business-critical platform.

- The Workday Ambassador should regularly attend major IT architecture and systems design meetings, where new technical solutions are being considered or implemented, as Workday should be the 'one source of truth' for employee data that nearly always feeds downstream business systems.

Remember the £37m spend in Part One that could have been deployed in Workday for £2m? This was a hard lesson learned!

Simple operational team structures with clear roles, accountability and responsibilities are key to success. Don't change for the sake of it; develop comprehensive and believable business cases with the senior leadership buy-in, and use Workday's free Value Proposition team. On each Workday release, squeeze every single drop of new functionality into your annual initiatives and future roadmaps – these small wins can add up and increase Workday adoption.

13

The Workday Ambassador

We've written extensively about how Workday has the potential to transform a business, and we've helped you navigate through the desert, so now there is hope on the horizon. We would also like to think that, having awoken an enthusiasm for what Workday might accomplish for you and your organisation, you could become its ambassador – if not you, a colleague who will pick up the baton and run with it. Because where there's a Workday will, there's a Workday way.

A Workday Ambassador is usually a senior leader from HR or finance who champions the whole Workday product. Ideally, this person reports to the Workday sponsor – ie the CPO who holds an active relationship with Workday, attends 'Workday Rising' and is the go-to person for all the global process owners (GPO) in the business.

We know from experience that having such a person on the inside is a vital factor in Workday's successful implementation and in ultimately helping to deliver both value and the all-important ROI. This is why we wanted to share with you at this point a named example of a Workday Ambassador in action: one of our clients who, we're proud to say, exemplifies all that we've written about in this book. We won't pretend it was always an easy ride for them, but it will show that the journey is worth it.

A natural agent of change

Jonathan Kohler (JK), Head of Change, Control and Governance for the CPO, was the Workday Ambassador for a Workday customer. Its global workforce amounts to 1,800, with 1,000 of those UK-based, 600 in Europe and the remainder scattered across smaller satellite offices. Small as the company is, it generates a significant volume of transactional data.

JK and his team looked after the change agenda, as well as all the controls in the functions – be that budget, risk events, compliance actions or the control environment. On the governance side, they managed the meeting cadence and the way that the HR senior management team functioned as a whole, ensuring that everyone involved stayed on topic and on track throughout the year to deliver on their promises to their clients. In these respects, JK ran the workhorse of the HR function.

Since being adopted into the business, Workday has become part of its DNA. JK knows from experience that this didn't happen overnight, and it took time for adoption to grow, but it reached a point where the other parts of the organisation beyond HR turned to Workday when they wanted to achieve certain outcomes. The finance team would now ask for specific integrated Workday data, when in the past they had relied on trying to merge spreadsheets that never fitted together in any satisfactory way. IT also now relied on Workday-generated data because they trusted its accuracy. The more JK guided the organisation through the three stages of Amplify, Augment and Analytics, the leaner and more efficient the data reporting became.

In 2016, when JK first joined the HR function, pre-Workday's introduction to the organisation, requesting data sets on demand from his HR colleagues was an arduous, knee-jerking process which brought about that all-too-familiar response: 'I'll get back to you'. Invariably, two weeks later he'd receive the previous month's management information (MI), which was already out of date. It was agreed that the organisation needed a system that would simply provide that information more quickly at the click of a button. That system was Workday.

JK's Workday journey started by looking at the most basic of HR systems – payroll data and spreadsheets. During an iterative journey, JK began to see change happen on an ever-increasing scale, from not quite believing in the first month whether the data was accurate, to thirty-six months down the line describing it to us as 'pretty transformational'. At the start, JK instinctively felt that Workday would be the answer, but because it's a premium subscription, he also knew he had to build the business case for it – which proved to be trickier and take longer than expected.

The turning point came with the arrival twelve months later of a new chief people officer who was already familiar with, and an advocate of, Workday. Once it went live, he faced two options:

1. Simply run it as an HR-focused system only

2. Take steps to ingrain it within the organisation's wider operations

JK suggested the latter and because he was an adopter from the beginning and was a natural change agent who understood its potential, he became the 'unofficial' official voice for Workday within the organisation and was keen to know how the business could better use it. He understood its architecture – its limitations at this early stage and its future potential. It fell to JK to become that person in meetings to suggest that they use Workday to integrate various processes, implement learning or form an advanced compensation process. Each time, JK would reinforce to the leadership the business case for Workday that he and his team had initially laid out. Such advocacy helped ingrain it into the team.

A holistic design

The GDA itself evolved into a more integrated design authority which wrapped around all their processes and changed where Workday was central to those conversations. For example, when they were considering a new employee engagement tool, the first thought was how it would integrate within Workday, and the second, how would data feed through the engagement tool; previously, the temptation might have been to purchase the engagement tool first and then work out how to make it fit with Workday. That shift in mindset from thinking of Workday as an afterthought to it being part of the organisation's DNA was critical to JK's advocacy of his change champion role at senior level.

JK and his team embarked on their decision-vision journey by streamlining their processes and making them efficient and meaningful. This allowed them to interpret data outcomes accurately so that the business could gauge where it sat within its competitive landscape, not only in terms of the market, but also in how it compared, through benchmarking, to its peer organisations. This helped JK's organisation, which in many respects was a traditional London insurance outfit, democratise the decision-making process between departments impacted by change, instead of continually relying on centralised directives.

Through the introduction of employee- and manager-led self-service, people became more proactive, having been given the tools to think further about the processes they owned but had never taken control of. HR was instrumental in coaching people to upskill themselves and adopt Workday and this changed the entire culture journey over a period of eighteen months. As part of an initiative called 'Work life better', that self-serve element extended into helping employees decide the right place for them to work and booking their own holidays. Giving people the ability to make adult choices was the beginning of this insurance company's culture journey and we assisted its continuous improvement initiatives.

As their customer integrator, our role was made far more seamless because JK was established as the Workday Ambassador who had engaged with its potential and was prepared to defend its business case to the executive. We had confidence in the SAHARA model standing up and delivering, and when the implementation went live, we helped JK tweak processes where adjustments inevitably needed to be made. When a backlog developed post-implementation, we spent time in the Authority stage looking at the critical red lines that would threaten the ROI if left untreated and misunderstood.

The SAHARA roadmap was essential to that, as was JK and his team's complete buy-in. This allowed us, as one unit, to examine the framework in detail. When we gave feedback to the executive, it confirmed they understood the ethos and the resultant value. That strict adherence to the GDA and governance enabled them to enter the Augment phase. From our perspective, advocacy is essential because only the client has the gravitas to understand their own business. Our job is to listen and respond, and so having a stakeholder on the inside really helps to bring Augment to life and make change happen.

Without a passionate champion at the heart of this journey, it's usually impossible to reach consensus, especially when the client is simply hoping that their SI partner will step in and take control – as we described in the 80/20 split. For JK's company, that was never the case, and since Workday's user adoption there is exceptionally high, the design authority has become its governance forum and its once-a-fortnight meeting is reportedly the best-attended by senior management. Its success lies in the fact that all attendees bring all their ideas to the table and are then interrogated to the Nth degree on how these will affect Workday.

JK's example is the gold standard of what HR functions need to aim for when it comes to Workday adoption, because both HR and Workday become one synergistic entity from which both intelligence and value grow. At its heart is culture, and therein lies its people. Driving that success is HR or finance pointing the compass needle in the right direction to lead the company out of the desert.

Conclusion

Now that we've guided you through the Workday journey and two parts of our 3A Blueprint, you have the model to deliver Workday's solutions more quickly, safely and cost-effectively than you previously imagined was possible, and we're confident you're in a better position to achieve the following outcomes:

- A cost-effective framework for serving your Workday users

- The knowledge to keep Workday updated and healthy

- The ability to align Workday with your business objectives and goals

It might have seemed daunting and unattainable at first, but now you have a concise and clear resource on hand to help you put these simple steps in place. We've put you back in control and, with our guiding hand, you can enable and empower your Workday users by giving them exactly what they need to do a fantastic job for your business.

We invite you to get started immediately because then you can begin to implement the simple elements that will create a dramatic impact. Use this guide to refresh your thinking and prompt you into action. Remember, there's no need to do this all on your own – leverage experts and your existing SI partners who fully understand the key things that you want to implement. This time, you are the one driving the process forward to meet the needs of your business.

In the introduction we referred to 'the hidden message' contained in this book. By now you'll have gathered that we believe none of the problems are solely attributable to Workday.

It's about the people.

When you combine people and Workday with the relevant expertise, something truly magical happens beyond Workday, your division and even yourself: it's transformative for your business.

Next steps

- If you haven't already, complete our short online Thriving on Workday Quiz at https://thrivingonworkday.scoreapp. com to discover where you are right now on your own Workday journey and learn which of the three steps needs your attention.

- Visit our website and portal at https:// lightwork.global/lw247 and download the helpful templates, accelerators and toolkits that can support you.

- Subscribe to our LinkedIn company page on which we share our insights into the latest Workday developments and releases: www.linkedin.com/company/ lightwork-global.

If you've benefited in any way from reading this book and want to contribute your own success stories, or ask us any questions, connect with us at www.lightwork.global/company/contact and together we'll help steer you away from the perils of straying into the desert.

Thank you for buying this publication and supporting the charities that benefit from the proceeds.

The Authors

Stephen Slevin

 Stephen has worked in both HR and payroll for over thirty years and has personally witnessed the evolution and growth of 'legacy people administrative systems' in the twentieth century, which gave birth to the new cloud-based HCM and business workflow solutions.

Stephen's entrepreneurial career began in 1998 when, aged twenty-nine, he founded his first textile business in collaboration with his mother, opened his first online retail store and sold to customers worldwide. Today this business operates in the UK, Europe and Australia and has more than 4,000 customers worldwide.

Stephen continues his entrepreneurial success via 'angel investing' in more than thirty start-ups and enjoys the passion and thrill of meeting new founders keen to develop their products and services which better the world we live in today.

In 2010, Stephen was introduced to Workday while living and working in Australia. He was fortunate to work on multiple Workday projects and certified through a Workday SI partner. This enabled him to grow his experience and knowledge, with direct support from Workday, over the following twelve years.

In June 2020, Stephen and Dan formed Lightwork Global because they both noticed a gap in the market for new ways to deliver Workday, with their primary focus being on the best outcomes and giving the customer more control of the business change transformation.

Stephen is active in fundraising for his chosen charity: Motor Neurone Disease Association.

in www.linkedin.com/in/stephenslevin

Daniel Dore

 Daniel Dore is an expert on digital change and transformation and a renowned specialist on quality assurance and testing. He has guided numerous companies through the transition to cloud-based SaaS solutions, transforming their digital operations and client-facing systems. His clients include the BBC, Lloyds Bank and Brewin Dolphin.

Today, Daniel is CEO of Assured Thought. Their specialists have worked on hundreds of successful change and transformation projects for their clients. They have received multiple awards and recognition from their industry peers for this.

Daniel is now a leading figure in his industry, and a professional writer and speaker on the topics of software quality and digital transformation.

In a world where companies struggle with complex IT, Daniel is passionate about simplicity. With his playbook of methods and tools to deliver meaningful outcomes for his clients, he helps them achieve success.

🌐 www.assuredthought.com

in www.linkedin.com/in/danieljdore